Electrofuels: The Next Generation of Carbon-Neutral Fuels

Contents

Preface
Introduction
Chapter 1: Introduction to Electrofuels
Chapter 2: How Electrofuels Work
Chapter 3: Types of Electrofuels
Chapter 4: Advantages of Electrofuels
Chapter 5: Challenges in Electrofuels Production
Chapter 6: The Role of Electrofuels in the Energy Transition
Chapter 7: Policy Support for Electrofuels
Chapter 8: Current Developments and Key Players
Chapter 9: Case Study: Electrofuels in Shipping
Chapter 10: Conclusion and Future Outlook

Glossary

Preface

The global push toward decarbonization is driving the search for sustainable alternatives to fossil fuels, and electrofuels are emerging as a key contender in this quest. Electrofuels, also known as synthetic fuels, are produced using renewable electricity, offering a carbon-neutral solution to meet energy demands across multiple sectors, including transportation and shipping.

Electrofuels: The Next Generation of Carbon-Neutral Fuels is part of the Gosships Learning Series, designed to provide professionals with a comprehensive understanding of this cutting-edge technology. Electrofuels promise to play a significant role in reducing greenhouse gas emissions, particularly in industries that are difficult to decarbonize. This book explores the science, technology, and market potential of electrofuels, equipping readers with the knowledge needed to engage with this transformative energy solution.

This series is designed to provide foundational to intermediate knowledge, focusing on practical applications and real-world relevance. Every book in this series is paired with a certification test, ensuring that the knowledge gained is not only understood but can be directly applied in professional settings.

We hope this book will serve as an essential guide for maritime and energy professionals looking to stay ahead of the curve in the evolving world of carbon-neutral fuels.

Introduction

Welcome to *Electrofuels: The Next Generation of Carbon-Neutral Fuels*, a deep dive into the innovative world of electrofuels, an emerging technology designed to meet global decarbonization goals. As the maritime and energy sectors seek sustainable alternatives to traditional fuels, electrofuels are gaining attention for their ability to provide low-carbon energy solutions. Derived from renewable electricity and carbon captured from the atmosphere, electrofuels offer a promising pathway to reduce greenhouse gas emissions without compromising energy needs.

This book covers the following key areas:

- **Understanding Electrofuels**: Learn the basics of what electrofuels are and how they are produced.

- **Production Pathways**: Explore the various methods of synthesizing electrofuels, including Power-to-Liquids and Power-to-Gas technologies.

- **Applications in Maritime and Other Sectors**: Examine how electrofuels can be integrated into maritime operations and other energy-intensive industries.

- **Economic and Market Considerations**: Dive into the costs, market potential, and economic factors shaping the future of electrofuels.

- **Environmental Impact**: Understand the sustainability benefits of electrofuels and their role in reducing global carbon footprints.

After reading this book, you will be prepared to take an assessment designed to test your comprehension of the material. Upon successful completion, you will receive a Certificate of Achievement by visiting www.gosships.com and accessing the training platform, demonstrating your expertise in this forward-looking field.

Who is this book for?

This book is designed for:

- Energy and maritime professionals exploring carbon-neutral fuel options.

- Engineers and scientists interested in understanding the technology behind electrofuels.
- Policy makers and regulatory personnel working on sustainable energy solutions.
- Students and aspiring professionals looking to build a foundation in renewable energy technologies.

By mastering the concepts in this book, you will be equipped to contribute to the global transition toward sustainable energy, leveraging the potential of electrofuels to decarbonize industries that rely on high-energy inputs.

Gosships Learning Series 2024/2025

1. Hydrogen: The Fuel of the Future
2. Green Ammonia: The Next Big Thing in Shipping
3. Decarbonizing Shipping: Pathways to Zero Emissions
4. Battery Technology for Industrial Applications
5. Carbon Capture and Storage: Can It Save the Planet?
6. Biofuels 101: Turning Waste into Energy
7. Understanding LNG (Liquefied Natural Gas)
8. Methanol as a Marine Fuel
9. Offshore Wind Energy: The Future of Renewable Power
10. Tidal and Wave Energy: Harnessing the Ocean
11. Electrofuels: The Next Generation of Carbon-Neutral Fuels
12. Energy Storage Systems for Grid Reliability
13. Hydrogen Fuel Cells for Transportation
14. Solar Energy Innovations: Beyond Solar Panels
15. Smart Grids: The Backbone of Future Energy Systems
16. Ammonia-Hydrogen Blends: A Dual Fuel Solution?
17. Nuclear Power: Small Modular Reactors for a Low-Carbon Future
18. Hydropower: The Oldest Renewable Energy Source
19. Decentralized Energy Systems: Microgrids for Resilience
20. Energy Efficiency Technologies for Industry
21. Hydrogen Production from Seawater
22. Fuel Cells for Maritime Applications
23. Geothermal Energy: Unlocking Earth's Heat
24. Future of EV Charging Infrastructure

25. Synthetic Fuels: Bridging the Gap to Decarbonization
26. Cybersecurity for Maritime and Offshore Operations
27. AI and Automation in Shipping and Logistics
28. Digital Twins in Maritime: Revolutionizing Asset Management
29. Risk Management in Offshore and Maritime Operations
30. Compliance with IMO 2020 Regulations
31. Sustainable Ship Design: Reducing Environmental Impact
32. Marine Renewable Energy: Wave, Tidal, and Offshore Wind Integration
33. Ballast Water Management Systems
34. Blockchain Technology in Shipping: Improving Transparency & Efficiency
35. Effective Supply Chain Management for Energy Industries
36. Leadership in the Energy Transition
37. Effective Crisis Management in Maritime Operations
38. Shipyard Safety Management Systems
39. Port State Control (PSC) Inspection Readiness
40. Remote Vessel Operations and Autonomous Shipping
41. Optimizing Fleet Performance with Data Analytics
42. Maritime Environmental Regulations: Staying Ahead of Compliance
43. Advanced Maintenance Strategies: Condition Monitoring & Predictive Maintenance
44. Global LNG Market: Trends and Opportunities
45. Incident Investigation in Maritime Operations
46. International Maritime Law: Key Concepts and Applications
47. Emergency Preparedness and Response for Offshore Oil & Gas

48. Energy Transition Strategies for Oil and Gas Companies

49. Maritime Drones: Applications and Safety Considerations

50. Effective Project Management in Offshore Energy Projects

All Rights Reserved Disclaimer

The contents of this book, including but not limited to all text, graphics, images, logos, and designs, are the intellectual property of Gosships LLC and are protected by copyright law. No part of this publication may be reproduced, distributed, transmitted, displayed, or modified in any form or by any means, including photocopying, recording, or other electronic or mechanical methods, without the prior written permission of the publisher, except in the case of brief quotations in critical reviews or articles.

The information contained within this book is for educational purposes only and is provided "as is" without warranty of any kind, either expressed or implied. The authors and publishers disclaim any liability for any direct, indirect, or consequential loss or damage arising from the use of the material in this book.

For permissions or inquiries, please contact: admin@gosships.com

© 2024 Gosships LLC. All rights reserved.

Chapter 1
Introduction to Electrofuels

In the race to decarbonize the global economy, industries face the challenge of reducing greenhouse gas (GHG) emissions while meeting the world's growing energy demands. Electrofuels, or **e-fuels**, present an innovative solution. These synthetic fuels are created by combining **renewable electricity** with captured **carbon dioxide (CO_2)** to produce fuels that can replace conventional fossil fuels in many sectors.

The production of electrofuels revolves around using clean energy from wind, solar, or hydropower to drive chemical reactions that result in liquid or gaseous fuels. What makes electrofuels particularly exciting is their potential to be **carbon-neutral**. By using CO_2 as a feedstock, electrofuels do not introduce new CO_2 into the atmosphere; they merely recycle existing CO_2, making them a key player in the shift to a sustainable, low-carbon future.

The transportation sector, particularly **aviation, shipping**, and **heavy-duty vehicles**, is one of the largest contributors to global CO_2 emissions. Unlike passenger vehicles, these industries face significant challenges in electrifying their operations, making electrofuels a crucial bridge in the transition to cleaner energy sources. This book will introduce you to the science, benefits, and challenges of electrofuels and explore their role in reducing carbon emissions.

Chapter 2
How Electrofuels Work

Electrofuels are produced through a multi-step process that involves renewable electricity, water, and carbon dioxide. The core of electrofuels is built around a process called **power-to-fuel** technology, where electricity is converted into chemical energy.

Step 1: Electrolysis

Electrolysis is the process that lies at the heart of electrofuel production. In electrolysis, an electric current is passed through water (H_2O) to split it into **hydrogen** (H_2) and **oxygen** (O_2). When the electricity used in this process comes from renewable sources (such as solar or wind power), the hydrogen produced is referred to as **green hydrogen**. Green hydrogen is a crucial building block for electrofuels because it can be used as a fuel on its own or combined with other elements to create synthetic fuels.

Step 2: Carbon Capture

To achieve carbon neutrality, the second key element in the electrofuel process is **carbon dioxide** (CO_2). CO_2 can be captured from two primary sources:

1. **Industrial Carbon Capture**: CO_2 emitted by power plants, factories, or other industrial processes can be captured before it escapes into the atmosphere.
2. **Direct Air Capture (DAC)**: DAC technologies remove CO_2 directly from the atmosphere, even in areas far from industrial activity.

The captured CO_2 is then combined with green hydrogen in the next stage of electrofuel production.

Step 3: Fuel Synthesis

With green hydrogen and captured CO_2 in hand, the final step is to synthesize these elements into fuels. This is achieved through a chemical process, often involving **catalysts**, that converts the hydrogen and CO_2 into hydrocarbons like **methanol**, **kerosene**, or **diesel**. The resulting electrofuels can be liquid or gaseous and are chemically similar to traditional fossil fuels, making them compatible with existing energy infrastructure.

Chapter 3

Types of Electrofuels

Electrofuels are a diverse family of fuels, each tailored to specific applications across different industries. Here are the main types of electrofuels:

1. E-Methanol

E-methanol is one of the most common electrofuels and is often used as a **marine fuel**. It can also be used as a chemical feedstock in a variety of industrial applications. E-methanol is appealing because it can be easily blended with conventional fuels and transported using existing infrastructure. In addition to being used in ships, it can also serve as a feedstock for producing chemicals and plastics, making it a versatile option.

2. E-Diesel

E-diesel is a synthetic version of traditional diesel. One of its greatest advantages is that it can be used in conventional diesel engines without any modifications, making it ideal for **trucks**, **buses**, and other heavy-duty vehicles. E-diesel is produced by combining green hydrogen with captured CO_2 through a **Fischer-Tropsch synthesis** process. This results in a fuel that burns cleanly, reducing emissions while maintaining the high energy density that diesel engines require.

3. E-Kerosene

E-kerosene is poised to become a critical fuel for the **aviation industry**. Modern aircraft engines are built to run on kerosene-based fuels, and e-kerosene offers a sustainable alternative that can be used in existing planes. As airlines and governments face growing pressure to reduce aviation-related emissions, e-kerosene stands out as one of the only viable carbon-neutral alternatives for long-haul flights, where batteries are too heavy and impractical.

4. Synthetic Natural Gas (SNG)

SNG is a gaseous electrofuel that can be used as a direct replacement for natural gas in power plants, heating systems, and vehicles. SNG is appealing because it can be distributed through the same pipeline network used for conventional natural gas, providing a seamless transition for utility companies and consumers alike.

Chapter 4
Advantages of Electrofuels

Electrofuels present several advantages over traditional fossil fuels and even some renewable energy solutions. Below are some of the main benefits:

1. Carbon Neutrality

The most significant advantage of electrofuels is their potential to be **carbon-neutral**. By capturing CO2 that would otherwise contribute to global warming and using renewable electricity, electrofuels offer a solution that balances out their emissions, creating a **closed carbon cycle**. Unlike fossil fuels, which introduce new carbon into the atmosphere, electrofuels recycle CO2.

2. Compatibility with Existing Infrastructure

Electrofuels are **drop-in fuels**, meaning they can be used in the same engines, pipelines, and refueling stations designed for fossil fuels. This makes them a highly attractive option for industries looking to decarbonize without making massive investments in new infrastructure. Ships, planes, and vehicles can switch to electrofuels without needing to overhaul their engines or fuel storage systems.

3. Energy Storage

One of the challenges with renewable energy sources like wind and solar is that they produce energy intermittently—only when the sun is shining or the wind is blowing. Electrofuels provide a way to store excess renewable energy. By converting surplus electricity into electrofuels, energy can be stored for later use, helping balance the grid and reducing reliance on fossil fuels during times when renewable power generation is low.

4. Reducing Dependence on Fossil Fuels

Electrofuels offer a sustainable alternative to fossil fuels, reducing reliance on non-renewable resources and mitigating the geopolitical risks associated with fossil fuel extraction and distribution. As countries seek energy independence, electrofuels can play a role in diversifying energy portfolios.

Chapter 5
Challenges in Electrofuels Production

Despite their promise, electrofuels face several challenges that need to be addressed to make them viable at scale.

1. High Production Costs

The process of producing electrofuels is **energy-intensive** and currently much more expensive than producing fossil fuels. Electrolysis, in particular, requires a significant amount of electricity, and while renewable energy costs are falling, the overall process remains costly. Moreover, the infrastructure for carbon capture and storage (CCS) is still developing, and widespread adoption of Direct Air Capture (DAC) technology remains limited due to its cost.

2. Energy Efficiency

Electrofuels are less energy-efficient compared to other renewable energy solutions, such as direct use of electricity in **battery-electric vehicles** (BEVs). Each stage of the production process—electrolysis, carbon capture, and fuel synthesis—results in energy losses. For example, by the time renewable electricity is converted into hydrogen, combined with CO_2, and then synthesized into fuel, the total efficiency is often lower than if the electricity were used directly.

3. Scale and Infrastructure

While electrofuels can be used in existing engines and refueling infrastructure, significant investment is still needed to **scale production**. The facilities required to produce green hydrogen, capture CO_2, and synthesize electrofuels are currently limited in number and geographic spread. Building up this infrastructure will require collaboration between governments, industries, and investors.

4. Availability of Renewable Energy

Electrofuels are only as green as the energy used to produce them. To be truly carbon-neutral, electrofuels must rely on **renewable energy sources** for electrolysis and fuel synthesis. In regions where renewables are not yet widespread, the production of electrofuels could still depend on fossil fuels, reducing their environmental benefits.

Chapter 6
The Role of Electrofuels in the Energy Transition

Electrofuels are expected to play a **complementary role** in the global energy transition. While **batteries** and **hydrogen** are leading the charge in electrifying passenger vehicles and short-haul transport, electrofuels are better suited to sectors where electrification faces technological and economic barriers.

1. Aviation

Aviation is one of the hardest sectors to decarbonize. Electric planes are still in their infancy, and batteries are too heavy for long-haul flights. E-kerosene offers a **drop-in solution** that can be used in existing aircraft, allowing airlines to reduce their carbon emissions without waiting for breakthroughs in battery technology.

2. Shipping

Global shipping is responsible for approximately **3% of global carbon emissions**. The industry has been slow to adopt low-carbon technologies, but the International Maritime Organization (IMO) has set ambitious targets for reducing emissions. **E-methanol** and **e-diesel** are emerging as viable alternatives to heavy fuel oils currently used in shipping.

3. Heavy-Duty Vehicles

Trucks, buses, and other heavy-duty vehicles are another area where electrofuels could make a significant impact. While battery-electric trucks are becoming more common, they still face limitations in range and charging times. **E-diesel** and **synthetic natural gas** (SNG) provide alternatives that allow these vehicles to maintain their long-haul capabilities while reducing emissions.

4. Industrial Processes

Beyond transportation, electrofuels can also be used in **industrial processes** that require high-temperature heat, such as **cement**, **steel**, and **chemical** production. These industries are among the hardest to decarbonize, and electrofuels offer a way to replace fossil fuels in these applications.

Chapter 7
Policy Support for Electrofuels

Government policies and international regulations are critical to advancing the development and deployment of electrofuels. Several policy measures are already in place or being considered to support the growth of this sector.

1. Carbon Pricing

Carbon pricing mechanisms, such as **carbon taxes** and **emissions trading systems (ETS)**, place a financial burden on companies that emit CO_2, making fossil fuels more expensive relative to carbon-neutral alternatives like electrofuels. These policies create economic incentives for industries to adopt cleaner fuels and technologies.

2. Renewable Fuel Mandates

Some countries and regions are introducing **renewable fuel mandates** that require a certain percentage of transportation fuels to come from renewable sources. For example, the European Union has set ambitious targets for the use of sustainable aviation fuels (SAFs) in the aviation industry, which includes electrofuels like e-kerosene.

3. Subsidies and Incentives

Governments are offering subsidies and financial incentives to companies investing in **green hydrogen** production, **carbon capture**, and **electrofuel technologies**. These incentives help offset the high costs of developing and scaling these technologies, making them more competitive with fossil fuels.

4. International Climate Agreements

International agreements, such as the **Paris Agreement**, are pushing countries to set ambitious targets for reducing greenhouse gas emissions. As part of these efforts, many countries are looking to electrofuels as a way to decarbonize hard-to-electrify sectors and meet their climate goals.

Chapter 8
Current Developments and Key Players

Several companies, research institutions, and governments are actively working on developing electrofuels. Here are a few of the key players leading the way:

1. Porsche and Siemens Energy

In 2020, **Porsche** and **Siemens Energy** announced a partnership to build a commercial-scale e-fuel production plant in **Chile**. The plant will use wind power to produce green hydrogen, which will then be combined with captured CO_2 to create e-methanol and e-gasoline. This project is part of Porsche's broader strategy to reduce its carbon footprint, particularly in motorsports and luxury vehicles.

2. Maersk

Maersk, one of the largest shipping companies in the world, has committed to achieving net-zero emissions by 2050. As part of this goal, the company has begun investing in **e-methanol-powered ships**. These vessels will use electrofuels to significantly reduce their emissions compared to traditional heavy fuel oil.

3. Climeworks

Climeworks is a Swiss company specializing in **Direct Air Capture (DAC)** technology. The company's DAC plants capture CO_2 directly from the air, which can then be used in the production of electrofuels. Climeworks is one of the leaders in the DAC field and has partnered with various companies to scale up its technology.

4. Power-to-X Projects

Power-to-X refers to the conversion of renewable electricity into various forms of energy, including electrofuels. Several Power-to-X projects are underway in **Europe**, **Asia**, and **North America**, with the goal of producing large-scale electrofuels for industrial and transportation use.

Chapter 9
Case Study: Electrofuels in Shipping

To better understand how electrofuels can be applied in the real world, let's examine the case of **Maersk**, a global leader in shipping. Maersk's fleet of vessels is responsible for significant CO2 emissions, but the company has set ambitious goals to reduce its carbon footprint. One of the key components of this strategy is the adoption of **e-methanol** as a marine fuel.

Maersk has placed orders for ships that will run on e-methanol, marking a significant step forward in the decarbonization of the shipping industry. These vessels will operate with significantly lower emissions compared to ships powered by heavy fuel oil (HFO), which is commonly used in the maritime sector.

The decision to adopt e-methanol is driven by several factors:

1. **Regulatory Pressure**: The International Maritime Organization (IMO) has set targets to reduce shipping emissions by 50% by 2050, making it necessary for companies like Maersk to explore alternative fuels.

2. **Compatibility**: E-methanol can be used in existing ship engines with minor modifications, making it an attractive option for companies looking to transition quickly.

3. **Supply Chain Flexibility**: Methanol is relatively easy to store and transport, and it can be produced from a variety of renewable sources.

By transitioning to e-methanol, Maersk is not only reducing its emissions but also positioning itself as a leader in sustainable shipping. This case study highlights how electrofuels can be integrated into **existing industrial operations** to achieve real-world decarbonization goals.

Chapter 10
Conclusion and Future Outlook

The future of **electrofuels** looks promising, but several challenges must be overcome before they can be deployed at scale. As the world continues to grapple with the effects of climate change, industries that rely on **liquid fuels** will need to find alternatives to fossil fuels. **Electrofuels** offer one of the most viable solutions for hard-to-electrify sectors like **aviation**, **shipping**, and **heavy industry**.

To accelerate the adoption of electrofuels, several factors will be critical:

- **Technological Advancements**: Improving the efficiency of electrolysis and fuel synthesis processes will be essential in lowering the cost of electrofuels.

- **Investment in Infrastructure**: Governments and private investors will need to fund the development of **carbon capture facilities**, **green hydrogen production plants**, and **electrofuel refineries**.

- **Policy Support**: Governments must continue to provide incentives and regulations that support the growth of the electrofuels industry, such as carbon pricing, renewable fuel mandates, and subsidies for green technologies.

In the coming years, electrofuels are expected to play an increasingly important role in **global energy systems**. Their ability to reduce emissions while leveraging existing infrastructure makes them a critical tool in the fight against climate change. By 2030, it is anticipated that electrofuels will become more cost-competitive, enabling industries to transition away from fossil fuels and toward a cleaner, more sustainable future.

Electrofuels are not a silver bullet, but they are a crucial part of the **energy transition**, particularly for sectors that cannot easily electrify. By continuing to invest in research, infrastructure, and policy development, we can unlock the full potential of electrofuels and pave the way for a carbon-neutral future.

Glossary - *Electrofuels: The Next Generation of Carbon-Neutral Fuels*

1. **Ammonia (NH_3)**: A carbon-neutral electrofuel used for energy storage and transportation, made from nitrogen and hydrogen.

2. **Anaerobic Digestion**: A process that breaks down organic material to produce biogas, which can be upgraded to electrofuels.

3. **Battery Electric Vehicle (BEV)**: A vehicle powered by electricity stored in batteries, often compared to electrofuels for transport.

4. **Biomass**: Organic material used as a feedstock in electrofuel production through gasification or fermentation.

5. **Carbon Capture and Storage (CCS)**: A technology used to capture and store carbon dioxide, which can then be used in electrofuel synthesis.

6. **Carbon Dioxide (CO_2)**: A greenhouse gas used as a feedstock in the production of electrofuels when captured from industrial emissions.

7. **Carbon Intensity**: The amount of CO_2 emitted per unit of energy produced, which electrofuels aim to minimize.

8. **Catalyst**: A substance used to speed up chemical reactions, essential in the production of electrofuels.

9. **Circular Economy**: An economic system aimed at eliminating waste by reusing materials, relevant to electrofuels in sustainable energy practices.

10. **Combustion**: The process of burning electrofuels to produce energy, often with zero net carbon emissions.

11. **Decarbonization**: The process of reducing carbon emissions, which electrofuels help achieve by replacing fossil fuels.

12. **Direct Air Capture (DAC)**: A method of capturing CO_2 directly from the atmosphere for use in electrofuel production.

13. **Electrochemical Reaction**: A chemical reaction driven by electricity, key to converting CO_2 and water into electrofuels.

14. **Electrolysis**: A process that uses electricity to split water into hydrogen and oxygen, used in the production of electrofuels.

15. **Energy Carrier**: A substance, like electrofuels, that can store and transport energy produced from renewable sources.

16. **Energy Density**: The amount of energy stored in a fuel, such as electrofuels, per unit volume or mass.

17. **Feedstock**: Raw materials, such as CO_2 and hydrogen, used to produce electrofuels.

18. **Fischer-Tropsch Synthesis**: A process that converts carbon monoxide and hydrogen into liquid hydrocarbons, used in electrofuel production.

19. **Gasification**: A process that converts organic material into syngas, which can be used to produce electrofuels.

20. **GHG (Greenhouse Gas)**: Gases like CO_2 that contribute to climate change, which electrofuels aim to reduce by replacing fossil fuels.

21. **Green Hydrogen**: Hydrogen produced using renewable electricity, a key component in the synthesis of electrofuels.

22. **Hydrocarbons**: Organic compounds made of hydrogen and carbon, the basic structure of electrofuels.

23. **Hydrogen (H_2)**: A key input in electrofuel production, generated through electrolysis of water.

24. **Industrial Symbiosis**: Collaboration between industries to use byproducts like CO_2 in electrofuel production.

25. **Kerosene**: A fossil fuel used in aviation, which can be replaced by synthetic electrofuels in sustainable aviation.

26. **Methanation**: The process of converting hydrogen and CO_2 into methane, an electrofuel used for energy generation.

27. **Methanol (CH_3OH)**: A common electrofuel made by combining CO_2 and hydrogen, used as a liquid fuel alternative.

28. **Molecular Conversion**: The process of converting molecules, such as CO_2 and hydrogen, into electrofuels using chemical reactions.

29. **Molecule-to-Molecule Technology**: Technology used to convert basic molecules like CO_2 and hydrogen into more complex electrofuels.

30. **Net-Zero Emissions**: A balance between emitting and absorbing CO_2, which electrofuels aim to achieve by reusing captured carbon.

31. **Oxidation**: A chemical reaction that involves the transfer of electrons, playing a role in electrofuel combustion.

32. **Oxygen (O2)**: A byproduct of electrolysis, where water is split into hydrogen (for fuel) and oxygen.

33. **Oxygenate**: A compound containing oxygen, like methanol, which improves the combustion efficiency of electrofuels.

34. **P2G (Power-to-Gas)**: A technology that converts surplus renewable electricity into gases, like hydrogen, for electrofuel production.

35. **P2L (Power-to-Liquids)**: A process that uses renewable electricity to convert water and CO2 into liquid electrofuels like methanol.

36. **Photovoltaics (PV)**: Solar power technology that generates electricity, which can be used to produce electrofuels.

37. **Renewable Electricity**: Electricity generated from sources like wind, solar, and hydro, used to produce carbon-neutral electrofuels.

38. **Renewable Hydrogen**: Hydrogen produced using renewable energy, critical to making electrofuels sustainable and carbon-neutral.

39. **Sabatier Reaction**: A chemical reaction that converts hydrogen and CO2 into methane, used in electrofuel production.

40. **Scaling**: The process of increasing electrofuel production capacity to meet growing energy demand.

41. **Sectors Hard to Decarbonize**: Industries like aviation, shipping, and heavy industry, where electrofuels offer viable carbon-neutral solutions.

42. **Sustainable Aviation Fuel (SAF)**: Carbon-neutral fuels derived from renewable sources, including electrofuels, for aviation use.

43. **Synthetic Fuels**: Fuels produced from renewable electricity and captured carbon, also known as electrofuels.

44. **Synergy**: The combined effect of different renewable technologies, such as electrofuels and carbon capture, leading to greater efficiency.

45. **Syngas**: A mixture of hydrogen and carbon monoxide produced from biomass or waste, used to synthesize electrofuels.

46. **Thermochemical Process**: A method of converting materials, such as biomass, into fuels using heat and chemical reactions.

47. **Transport Sector**: One of the largest contributors to GHG emissions, where electrofuels offer an alternative to conventional fossil fuels.

48. **Zero Emission Vehicle (ZEV)**: A vehicle that produces no tailpipe emissions, which can run on electrofuels or batteries.

49. **ZEV (Zero-Emission Vessel)**: Ships that use electrofuels or other sustainable energy sources to operate without emitting greenhouse gases.

50. **Zero-Emission Energy**: Clean energy that produces no greenhouse gas emissions during operation, a key advantage of electrofuels.

www.ingramcontent.com/pod-product-compliance
Lightning Source LLC
Chambersburg PA
CBHW030109230526
45471CB00003B/1335